very small
LIVING
SPACES

very small LIVING SPACES

Design and Decorating Strategies
to Make the Most of What You Have

BY BETH FRANKS

HENRY HOLT AND COMPANY
NEW YORK

A FRIEDMAN GROUP BOOK

Published by Henry Holt and Company, Inc.,
115 West 18th Street,
New York, New York 10011

Library of Congress Cataloging-in-Publication Data
Franks, Beth
   Very small living spaces.
   Includes index.
   1. Room layout (Dwellings)   2. Interior decoration.
3. Personal space.   4. Space (Architecture)   I. Title.
NK2113.F68   1988   728   87-45993
ISBN 0-8050-0520-X

First Edition

VERY SMALL LIVING SPACES
was prepared and produced by
Michael Friedman Publishing Group, Inc.
15 West 26th Street
New York, New York 10010

Editor: Tim Frew
Designer: Marcena J. Mulford
Art Director: Mary Moriarty
Photo Editor: Christopher Bain
Production Manager: Karen L. Greenberg

Printed in Hong Kong

1   3   5   7   9   10   8   6   4   2

ISBN 0-8050-0520-X

Dedication

To my parents, Jean and Jerry, and sisters, Katie and Sue, who taught me how to maintain a balance between too many possessions and not enough space, one secret of living happily in a small home.

Acknowledgements

I'd like to thank Kathleen Poer, of Spacial Design in San Francisco, and DAK, of Koch Landmark Developments in Cincinnati, for sharing their design expertise. Thanks also to Judith Miley, of Clairson International, for research leads, and to the many manufacturers who provided product literature and photographs. Special thanks to my editor, Tim Frew, for trimming verbiage and straightening out structural problems in the manuscript, and to Marcy Mulford, for her help with the captions. Finally, I'm grateful for my friends, Maya, Sara, and Matt, who provided entertainment and emotional support throughout the writing process.

CONTENTS

INTRODUCTION

If you live in an apartment, condominium, or small house you probably feel squeezed for space. Since many of yesterday's mid-size apartments have been divided into today's efficiencies, more and more people have had to make do with small, oddly-shaped living spaces. The L-shaped apartment that has no walls to separate the sleeping area and the kitchen, the space with high ceilings and an irregular floor, the one-bedroom in a converted factory that has no entrance foyer and a sink and shower in the living area—all of these examples create perplexing design dilemmas.

VERY SMALL LIVING SPACES will help you find creative solutions to your design problems. Chapter One guides you through the planning stages: deciding on space priorities, determining the amount of usable space you have, and drawing up a workable floor plan. There are also strategies for making a space seem larger, and advice on coordinating elements such as color, texture, and scale.

Chapter Two explores the many options for structuring a small space, for all kinds of uses. You'll discover that a space can often serve dual-purposes: a closet may open up into a playroom for a child, a dining table may fold into a desk, and a platform or loft can serve as both a sleeping and lounging area. Chapter Three takes a look at ten case studies—people who've created exemplary environments structured to suit their individual living and working needs. Finally, at the end of the book, there is a comprehensive list of sources—manufacturers, retailers, and organizations that feature products or services of special interest to the small-space dweller.

Today's lifestyles encourage mobility, independence, and flexibility, and living spaces reflect this. No one book can supply all the answers, but with the ideas in VERY SMALL LIVING SPACES, you can design an environment that's efficient, beautiful, and tailored to your own needs. With thorough planning and a little ingenuity, living in a small space can be a very comfortable experience.

Chapter One

PLANNING AND ASSESSING LIVING NEEDS

E. Allen McGee/FPG Intl.

More and more people are opting to live in small homes or apartments because of economics or location. Yet trying to fit all your living needs into a limited area with taste and style is no easy task, even for the design-conscious decorator. Certain universal necessities—dining, sleeping, bathing, storage, seating, entertaining—must have their place, but trying to fit them all into a studio apartment can create a chaotic, claustrophobic atmosphere.

Organizing a small space has a lot to do with creating an illusion of more rather than less. Finding every last inch of space in a small home or apartment and using it efficiently and comfortably is the crux of this organization. Throughout this book, we'll be looking at ways to create affordable and accessible, yet luxurious living spaces.

The first step is to take a good hard look at what you've got to live with. Think about how you want your living space to function: Are you a weekend parent who needs a place for the kids to stay? Do you entertain? Do you work out with weights at home? Once you've assessed your needs, it is much easier to devise imaginative solutions to transform your small space into a completely functional and beautiful dream home.

Form Follows Function

Before you draw up a plan and start rearranging furniture—or walls—on paper, it's important to decide on your space priorities. Often, rooms are used for more than one activity, so you need to decide which function is most important. For instance, assume you have the luxury of a spare bedroom. You like having it available to use as a guest room, but you also want to set up a home office where you can write the great American novel at night and on weekends. Since you have guests only once or twice a year, it makes sense to make the room primarily an office, with a daybed, Murphy bed, or some other "disguised" treatment for the secondary function of guest room. On the other hand, if you often have guests from out of town, but have only one bedroom, you might want to designate "guest room" as the living room's primary function. Deep banquette seating converts to a single bed in nothing flat, as do some futon frames. There are also ottomans designed to open up into beds. For a double bed "couch," use a futon frame, or try the classic solution, a sofa bed.

© Derrick & Love 1987

This room's primary function is dining, and it even features two options: a table and a countertop breakfast area. Yet it gracefully incorporates a living area that adapts to both sitting and sleeping, thanks to the deep banquettes.

This kitchen is a model of cleverly utilized space. Cabinets go almost all the way to the ceiling, and the cantilevered counter serves triple duty for food preparation, dining, and storage. The work island incorporates a sink and allows several people to work in the kitchen without stepping on each other's toes.

Living and dining are frequent cohabitors—a large plant and a strategically placed chair are all that separate this dining area from the living room. Placing a table on the diagonal helps make a small room seem larger by breaking up the space in an unexpected way.

Maybe you have a small kitchen that also features a dining area. If you love to cook, but hate the lack of counter space, consider remodeling the kitchen to include more cabinets and a cantilevered counter that can also be used for dining. Or you might decide to sacrifice the secondary function of eating in the kitchen to make it a more efficient work area. Or perhaps you love to give large, sit-down dinner parties, but lack a formal dining room. It may be possible to create an elegant dining space in your living room, using a combination of collapsible tables and coffee tables that can be raised to dining height.

If you live in a studio apartment, you need to define the main activity areas and create zones within the one room. In a large studio, standing screens, wall units, and even pull-down shades can be used to divide space. Decide which basic activities to combine—sleeping/sitting, cooking/eating, eating/entertaining, or sitting/entertaining. Some activities don't naturally seem to go together, but can still be successful collaborators. For instance, an artist may use a 3-by-14½ foot (.9-by-4.4 meter) table for working, eating, displaying artwork or books, and even sleeping (with a mat). Underneath the table is extra space for books and storage. Obviously only you can decide what is really important to you. The most important point is to think about how you use your

Living and sleeping are another natural combination provided the "bed" is at least partially disguised. A hammock can be used for everyday lounging as well as for occasional overnight guests.

available space. List your main preferences, then brainstorm possibilities as to how to adapt your home to fit.

As you think about all the uses that a room has to perform, also consider how often it's used for each. If the uses are fairly concurrent (you sleep in the living room, for instance), you need a flexible setup, something that's easily transformed. Also think about what furnishings, accessories, and artwork you have, and what you want to keep in each room. You'll probably find that

you want to get rid of some stuff, and that there are other things you'd like to buy.

Consider your habits too. Do you want a room to accommodate your habits or change them? For instance, if you have perpetual piles of papers on the floor—ongoing projects and a sort of ''visual'' filing system—you must first decide whether you want to eliminate those piles, get them out of sight, or keep them in the open for easier access. The options are as simple as a file cabinet or cupboard for closed storage, and

open shelving, a table, or desk top for accessibility.

Finally, think about the emotional effect of the room. How would you like to feel when you're occupying this particular space? For instance, if you wake up and exercise in a room, you may want to fill it with warm colors (reds, oranges); whereas, if you use a room to unwind after work, cool colors (blues, greens) might be better. (See page 28 for more on the use of color.)

You are the architect of your destiny when it comes to your home—you can create an environment that's uniquely yours. And in searching for viable treatments of problem spaces, you may be surprised at what you come up with—sometimes the simplest solutions are right under your nose.

Left: Studio apartments call for imaginative, flexible use of space—everything must work together to create a harmonious effect. This apartment uses the three central support beams as natural dividers while unifying the separate areas with color and artwork. *Facing page*: This is the same apartment viewed from the opposite end. Decorating tricks are essential in studios. White walls make the space seem to expand while the brown beams pull the eye upward, enhancing the height of the room.

Designer: Roberta Pincus/Photos (2): Bill Rothschild

Does It Measure Up?

Once you have a general idea of how you want your space to function, you need to find out exactly how much floor you are working with. Using a coil spring tape measure to insure accuracy, measure the length, width, and height of all the rooms, taking into account doors and windows, as well as protrusions such as radiators and elaborate moldings. Note any architectural features as well: fireplaces, alcoves, arched openings, built-ins, sliding or folding doors.

Also measure the closets. Most likely a lot of wasted space is lurking in there that you'll eventually want to exploit. If you want to be really thorough, make note of all electrical outlets, light switches, and telephones. While you're at it, pay attention to available wall space. A wall unit, high shelves, or cupboards to the ceiling may be just what you need to expand available floor space. With minor construction, kitchen soffits can be removed for additional storage space, or the space between wall studs can be knocked out to create shallow shelves or cupboards.

Write your measurements in feet and inches, rather than inches alone, to avoid errors. (Does not pertain to the metric

Above: When measuring your space, take architectural features into account and think of ways to use them to best advantage. A shallow alcove is the focal point of this room thanks to a couch that fits snuggly inside. The alcove also acts as a large "frame" for the artwork.

Left: Use wall space for everything it's worth. This wall unit exploits the entire wall, from floor to ceiling, for housing storage, an entertainment center, and a workspace.

Above: Placing a large plant in the corner of a room and then shining a light up through its leaves will make the corner seem to disappear as well as create interesting patterns on the ceiling and walls.

Facing page: A few large pieces of furniture are actually better than smaller scale furnishings in a small space. This bulky sofa, placed against the wall, makes the room look longer; the rug also promotes this illusion.

system.) These dimensions will be the "blueprint" that enables you to play with the space without making expensive mistakes. When working with a plan, you may see immediately if the room is out of balance. You can play with the pieces you already own, as well as things you'd like to add, and you can figure out the best bets for remodeling or structural alteration.

Using these measurements, draw up a plan, to scale, of your existing space. Use graph paper that's divided into ¼-inch (6 millimeter) squares. Using a scale of ¼ inch to a foot, draw the outlines of the space in dark pencil or pen, leaving spaces for windows, doors, and protrusions. Any special features, such as built-in bookshelves or projecting columns, should be carefully drawn to scale. Then make symbols for your existing furniture, as well as any pieces you would like to buy. These don't have to be the exact shape as the real thing, but should be as close to scale as possible. (Yes, this means you'll need to measure the furniture too.) Cut out the furniture templates from light cardboard or heavy paper so you can move them around on the plan to find the best arrangement. Another method is to use onionskin or tracing paper as an overlay, sketching in various arrangements. Draw freehand until you settle on the final plan, then use a ruler to render the shapes more precisely. Likewise, if you opt for cardboard templates, once you finalize the floor plan, trace around the symbols to record the layout.

When arranging furniture, start with the most important piece. Separate large pieces so the room doesn't become unbalanced. In a very small room it's usually best to position large or bulky furniture—large sofas, heavy wood pieces, armoires, etc.—against a wall. Placing them in the middle of the room makes the furniture look bigger and the room smaller. Consider natural traffic patterns, and allow at least forty inches (one meter) for major pathways. If possible, arrange seating in a way that allows traffic to move around the grouping, not through it. A U-shape is one of the best ar-

Designer: Denise Balassi Assoc. Photo: Bill Rothschild

rangements to seat a lot of people in a small space.

The plan will show how much furniture can be included in one room, and where. But don't settle on the first arrangement that comes to mind. Since you don't have to drag real furniture around the room, brainstorm many options. Also, experiment with new furniture on paper: How would a wall unit work to divide the living and dining areas? Would a modular banquette solve your seating problems, or create a crowded feeling? Is there room for a rolling work island in the kitchen? Once you finalize your decisions, your plan will act as a buying guide.

It may also be possible to vary the existing layout of a home without making major structural alterations. For instance, you could construct a raised platform with a pull-out bed, on casters, underneath. Or if you have high ceilings, it may be possible to construct a loft without attaching it to the walls. Bolted and screwed together, it can be disassembled and taken with you when you move. Use your plan to explore the possibilities—built-in storage, an office/closet, a bed on pulleys that lowers from the ceiling, a fold-down table, a sleeping loft, whatever. Then work with a designer or carpenter to make sure your great ideas are viable.

While you should finish reading this book before settling on a final arrangement, it is good to start planning right away. Study what you like in these pages and in magazines, showrooms, and the homes of your friends. Look at what works—and what doesn't. Also pay attention to what attracts you: furnishings, fabrics, color, texture, or some "special touch." All of these elements are important in creating a jewel of a small space.

Finally, photocopy your plan and carry it and a tape measure with you at all times. That way if you're out shopping and you unexpectedly come across the couch of your dreams on sale, you'll know by its measurements whether it's really perfect after all.

fitted spreads and lots of pillows that help create the illusion of a couch, some have an additional mechanism that converts the couch into two beds. Daybeds are similar, the only difference being a decorative frame that includes a railing or raised barrier at the foot and head. A daybed functions as a sofa when placed against a wall and piled with pillows, but usually tends to look more like a bed than a couch.

Sofa beds and convertible ottomans come in a variety of styles, but some are more suitable for full-time use than others. Some sofa bed mattresses are so thin that you can feel the metal frame supporting the bed. After a few nights of that, the floor will begin to look inviting! If you plan to sleep in a convertible bed on a regular basis, look for a mattress at least three inches (8 centimeters) thick.

Futon frames convert from couch to bed in the blink of an eye. Lightweight and comfortable, futons are usually five to ten inches (13 to 26 centimeters) thick and are great for daily use. Arise Futon's Cloud Nine model has a 2-inch (5-centimeter) layer of high-compression, high-density foam at the core of its cotton batting layers, which makes sleep a heavenly experience.

The Murphy bed is the ultimate camouflage treatment. Thanks to a spring-operated, counter-balancing mechanism, the bed folds up flat against the wall, literally disappearing into a cabinet or closet when not in use. Continually improved since 1900, Murphy beds come in models suitable for everyday or occasional use and will accommodate twin, double, queen, and king size mattresses. They require twelve to fifteen inches (31 to 38 centimeters) of recess space with cabinetry ranging from simple bi-fold doors to complete wall systems.

If you have high ceilings, a loft bed will utilize wasted vertical space as well as add visual interest. The space under the bed can be used for working, dining, or storage. You can also reverse the functions and sleep on floor level while using the loft for another activity. Allow about seven feet (2 meters) of head clearance for a loft that requires room to stand under, five feet (1.5 meters) for seating, and four feet (1.2 me-

ters) for sleeping. Loft beds are usually custom-built; however, a few prefabricated models are also available. The best place to install a loft is at the narrow end of an area, where the side walls can help support it. Since heat rises, lofts should be open on both sides at the upper level for better circulation.

Another possibility is to have a waist-high wooden platform custom-built for your space, with a mattress for sitting and

sleeping on top, and plenty of storage drawers underneath. Or if your living space is delineated by low ''conversation group'' platforms, bed units can be constructed to slide out like drawers.

If you take a guerrilla approach to decorating, you might like the simplest sleeping arrangement of all: a hammock. Strung between hooks in the corner of a room, it can act as seating in the daytime or

© Lynn Karlin 1987

James R. Levin/FPG Intl.

Left: The antique custom of enclosing a bed with draperies is reborn in this modern studio apartment.
Facing page: A loft bed frees up the usually wasted space under the bed.

be taken down when not in use. Mexican hammocks, handmade in the Yucatan, are designed to be slept in—the intricate network of lightweight strings gives a lot of support without digging into you as rope hammocks tend to do. Yucatan hammocks are colorful and roomy: *El matrimonio* sleeps two comfortably. Measure your space before drilling any holes, as hammocks are usually longer than they ap-

pear, and be sure to anchor hooks securely into the wall studs, or else you will be in for a rude awakening.

Since you don't need much headroom to sleep, small, low areas can also serve well. Attics and eaves can be converted into cozy bedrooms. In an alcove, a bed can be hidden in the daytime behind a pull-down shade, curtain, or standing screen. (For a ''hidden'' bed in the middle of a room,

construct a frame and hang draperies of transparent muslin or net to surround the bed.)

For guests, consider all of the above options, plus the less glamorous: army cots, sleeping bags, and air mattresses. Guests need a modicum of quiet and privacy, plus access to a bathroom, but given that, extra sleeping quarters can be improvised in the dining room, living room, an alcove, or even in a wide hallway.

Eating

The dining room seems to be a casualty of the space crunch of recent years. Fewer and fewer apartments have a room devoted solely to eating. People who do have this luxury often find themselves using the room for an office or something besides dining. In one-bedroom and studio apartments, the dining area is often an L-shaped extension of the living area, adjacent to the kitchen, and must be compatible with both.

Your setup here will depend on your priorities and situation. Does your family eat dinner together every evening, or do you live alone and dine out five nights a week? Do you sometimes throw parties for twenty-five or more people? You need to decide exactly how much emphasis you want to place on dining, relative to your space.

If eating at home is an off and on thing with you, your dining area can melt unobtrusively into another area by means of a fold-down table that disappears against the wall when not in use, or a work table that gets cleared off to use for dining. On the other hand, if sharing food is a joy that deserves space in your life, a dining area can be defined within a room in various ways: with lights (candles, spot or track lights, a chande-

A fold-down table increases this small kitchen's flexibility since it can serve as both an eating and a work surface. Streamlined tractor-seat stools consume very little visual space.

lier); with a room divider (a bookcase or wall unit set in the middle of the room, or curtains or standing screens that can be pulled around the table to create intimacy); or with a large area rug.

The main thing that defines a dining area is the table. A round, pedestal-base table seats a lot of people while also creating an illusion of space. Neither the eye nor your legs are encumbered by excess furniture supports (i.e., table legs). Glass topped tables also tend to look smaller. Cantilevered chairs are good for the same reason: They don't stop the eye with their bulk, and extra legs are eliminated. Using track lights instead of a chandelier in a dining area also promotes the illusion of space.

Table options can be as varied as sleeping arrangements. There are console tables that expand with the addition of leaves. Many models now provide self-storage of extra leaves, which solves the eternal problem of what to do with them when you aren't expecting dinner guests. Some models fold up into large squares, and even feature storage for extra folding chairs. Some coffee tables are adjustable to as many as five different levels, so you can raise them up to dining height whenever the need arises. Other collapsible tables with beautiful tops are designed to be stored on the wall as "art." Although these options are most often used in entertainment situations, they still may work for you on an everyday basis if eating at home isn't a high priority. Always test collapsible, adjustable, and folding tables for sturdiness before purchasing, because they can be shaky. Also check to see how easily they can be put up and taken down, or, in the case of adjustable height tables, how easily raised from level to level.

In a studio or L-shaped space, a banquette with seating on both sides of a shared back could serve for both the dining and living areas. Deep storage bins in the base of the

Dining and cooking areas naturally flow into one another in this small home, which makes serving and cleaning up after meals a breeze.

Courtesy Poggenpohl

banquette hold rarely used items. A folding picnic table works in a very narrow area.

For entertaining, create an instant dining room in the corner of the living room, work room, bedroom, or even the front porch. When additional eating surfaces are needed, a folding table is one of the simplest solutions. Or use a table with an expanding top, either separately or placed next to a table of the same height to create one big table. Two narrow tables, normally placed side by side against a wall, can be pulled out into the room and put together to seat up to six people. Snack tables can be used singly or arranged in groups to form a dining area. In a pinch, two permanent surfaces—a desk and a large end table, for instance—can each be set for large dinner parties.

Extra seating can take the form of stools, benches, folding or stacking chairs, floor pillows, banquettes, or couches. The most important thing to remember when improvising dining arrangements is that seating must be scaled to the table height. For instance, if you use occasional chairs, which are usually lower than dining room chairs, the table must be proportionately lower as well. Of if you prefer to eat Japanese style, sitting on the floor, pillows will bring guests up to coffee table height.

Above: The "trolley table," which parks under a counter, can be rolled into the combination dining room/living room for formal dining or over to the window seat, as shown here. Arched ceiling moldings suggest an arbor and help give the kitchen its English country flavor. (See page 38 for a look at the living/dining room.)

Facing page: Until homeowners decided to tear down walls for more open space, this multipurpose kitchen was two separate tiny rooms and a hallway. The window seat at left, with the railing in place, doubles as a playpen.

Courtesy Armstrong, Solarian Supreme/Gilliam Furniture

Cooking

The needs of an efficiency kitchen are quite different from those of a kitchen used for turning out elaborate gourmet meals. Think about how you use your kitchen, as well as how you want it to function. Do you feel like you're running an obstacle course every time you fix dinner? Is traffic routed straight through your work area? Would a work island give you the extra counter and storage space you crave?

Kitchens are the most often remodelled rooms in the house, with Americans spending $17.8 billion annually on renovations and changes. Inefficient work areas, inadequate counter and cabinet space, lack of electrical outlets, poor lighting and ventilation are the most frequent problems cited by dissatisfied homeowners. But if you're stuck with a small kitchen and remodelling is out of the question, storage is one secret of success. With your priorities clearly established, storage can be organized into a streamlined system and tailored to your needs.

Base your system on the point-of-first-use principle: Anything you use often should be easy to get your hands on, while less used items don't deserve prime space. For instance, if you stir fry once a week, your cleaver, wok, and sesame oil should be within an arm's reach. If you use your food processor daily, store it on the counter. If you entertain often, your fine china, crystal, table linens, and silver should be easily accessible; whereas if you have company only a couple of times a year, your stemware could be stored on the very top shelf of the cupboard. Think about how you operate in your kitchen and what's going to be most convenient for YOU, then arrange your storage accordingly.

If your space is limited, you really can't afford to store anything you don't need. Give

Courtesy St. Louis Group/Build Inc. Photographer: Jim Hedrich

Courtesy Armstrong, Solarian II/Headliner, Bravada

Collector

Almost any collection can be displayed: stamps, butterflies, coins, and more can be framed and hung on the wall; antique furniture can be integrated into a room's floorplan; dolls, shells, and rocks can be arranged on shelves or in glass cases. A high shelf spanning the top of the room is a time-honored solution for collections of objects. This antique library card catalog is a great idea for storing audio cassettes or compact discs.

Home Computer Center

A work station that wraps around a corner provides a lot of room for writing, typing, and keyboarding. A chair on casters allows freedom of movement from one area to another, making files and storage cabinets highly accessible. The white laminate blends in with the walls, making the space seem larger, while overhead cabinets take advantage of what could be wasted space.

© Michael A. Keller 1987/FPG Intl.

Courtesy Techline   By Marshall Erdman and Associates

Designer: Allyn Kandel/Photo: Bill Rothschild

Student Room

Many students must combine study, living, and sleeping space. This can be quite a balancing act, but making the bed do double duty as a couch is one simple solution. A light-colored, wraparound wall unit combining storage with work spaces unifies the room and makes it appear larger.

© Peter Gridley 1987/FPG Intl.

Raising a Family

Bunk beds are a space-saving solution for kids who must share a small room. Open and hanging storage of books and toys makes it easy for kids to clean up after themselves. The large window allows the eye to travel up and out, making the room feel bigger.

This family created a living area by using seating to segregate a corner of their large all-purpose room. The shelf under the window and wall mounted bookcase provide decorative storage.

Courtesy Velux-America Inc.

Home Recording Studio

Designer Richard D. Lawrence and audio consultant Holly Neil created a custom home audio and recording system for this songwriter. Bi-fold doors conceal reel-to-reel tape recorders, tuner, equalizer, cassette decks, album and tape storage, while the turntable is displayed in the mirrored recess.

A custom switch panel allows the songwriter to expedite dubbing and duplicating in four directions on either tape format, and to regulate speaker control throughout the second floor.

A wall of ash cabinetry conceals the kitchen audio system; cabinet interiors are automatically illuminated when the doors are opened. The Technics Linear Tracking turntable is raised on an angle for easier operation.

SOURCES

American Institute of Architects
1735 New York Avenue NW
Washington, DC 20006
(202) 626-7300
Information on local chapters and
state societies of AIA

American Society of Interior Designers
1430 Broadway
New York, NY 10018
(212) 944-9220
Information on local chapters of ASID

Amisco Industries Ltd.
P.O. Box 250
L'Islet, QUE
Canada GOR-2CO
(418) 651-3227
Furnishings

Arise Futon Mattress Co., Inc.
57 Green Street
New York, NY 10012
(212) 925-0310
Futons

Armstrong World Industries, Inc.
P.O. Box 3001
Lancaster, PA 17604
(717) 397-0611
Flooring, furnishings

Atelier International Ltd.
30-20 Thomson
Long Island City, NY 11101
(718) 392-0300
Furnishings

Beylerian Ltd. (see also Vecta Contract)
305 East 63 Street
New York, NY 10021
(212) 755-6303
Furnishings, storage systems

Binova Kitchens
995 Arrow Road
Toronto, ONT
Canada M9M-2Z5
(416) 749-5102
Kitchen cabinetry and furnishings

Black & Decker
U.S. Household Products
6 Armstrong Road
Shelton, CT 06484
(203) 926-3000
Under-cabinet appliances

Building and Design Resource Center
Designer's Walk
168 Bedford Road
Toronto, ONT
Canada M5R-2K9
(416) 961-8577
Information center and resource library

California Closet Company
6409 Independence Avenue
Woodland Hills, CA 91367
(818) 888-5888
Closet systems

Canadian Closet Company
210 Donpark Road
Markham, ONT
Canada L3R-2V2
(416) 477-0581
Custom closet systems

Castro Convertibles Corporation
1990 Jericho Turnpike
New Hyde Park, NY 11040
(516) 488-3000
Convertible furniture

Closet Maid
Clairson International
720 South West 17th Street
Ocala, FL 32674
(800) 437-7276
Closet systems

Contempora Designs International Inc.
887 Yonge Street
Toronto, ONT
Canada M4W-2H2
(416) 964-9295
Furnishings and lighting

Contract Design Centre
21 Water Street
Vancouver, B.C.
Canada V6B-1A1
(604) 681-5371
Contract Italian furnishings

DeBoer's
5051 Yonge Street
Willowdale, ONT
Canada L5L-1C7
(416) 226-3730
Furnishings and accessories

Decoret Wall Systems Plus
1017 Clement Street
San Francisco, CA 94118
(415) 668-6066
Wall systems

Design Zone
315 Danforth Avenue
Toronto, ONT
Canada M4K-1N7
(416) 462-1875
Furnishings

Fidelity Products
5601 International Parkway
P.O. Box 155
Minneapolis, MN 55440
(612) 536-6500
Office storage and supplies

General Electric Co.
Louisville, KY 40225
(800) 626-2000
Space-saving appliances

Heller Designs, Inc.
41 Madison Avenue
New York, NY 10010
Closet grids, record racks

Home Shelving
180 Steeles Avenue West
Thornhill, ONT
Canada L4J-2L1
(416) 881-9220
Shelving, storage systems

Horizon International
1225 Connecticut Avenue, NW
Suite 315
Washington, DC 20036
(202) 223-6166
Entertainment storage systems

ICF (International Contract
Furnishings, Inc.)
305 East 63rd Street
New York, NY 10021
(212) 750-0900
Furnishings

International Centre of Design
& Decoration of Montreal
85 Rue St. Paul Ouest
Montreal, QUE
Canada H2Y-2K7
(514) 842-4545
Furnishings and resources

Industrial Revolution/
Closet on Wheels
20 Hazelton Avenue
Toronto, ONT
Canada M5R-2E2
(416) 968-2599
Storage systems

Ikea Incorporated
Plymouth Commons
Plymouth Meeting, PA 19462
(215) 834-0150
Furnishings, organizing products

Julie's Interiors
1563 Dundas Street West
Mississauga, ONT
Canada L5C-1E3
(416) 275-3841
Furnishings and
design consultation

J Wood
P.O. Box 367
Route 322
Milroy, PA 17063
(717) 667-3961
Cabinetry for kitchen and bath

Kartell USA
P.O. Box 1000
Easley, SC 29641
(800) 845-2517
Furnishings, accessories

Kohler Company
444 Highland Drive
Kohler, WI 53044
(414) 457-4441
Bath and kitchen hardware

Lee/Rowan
6333 Etzel Avenue
St. Louis, MO 63133
(800) 325-6150
Closet organizers and accessories

Lockwood
1187 Third Avenue
New York, NY 10021
(212) 772-9400
Wall systems and furnishings

Mississauga Home and Design Center
2575 Dundas Street West
Mississauga, ONT
Canada L5K-2M6
(416) 828-1162
Thirty specialty stores

Murphy Door Bed Co., Inc.
5300 New Horizons Boulevard
Amityville, NY 11701
(516) 957-5200
Murphy beds

New Moon
561 Windsor Street
Somerville, MA 02143
(800) 343-4019
Futons and futon furniture

Nienkamper
415 Finchdene Square
Scarborough, ONT
Canada M1X-1B7
(416) 298-5700
Furnishings

NuTone Inc.
Madison and Red Bank Roads
Cincinnati, OH 45227
(513) 527-5100
Built-in ironing and food
processing centers

Organization USA
1755-C Wilwat Drive
P.O. Box 861
Norcross, GA 30091
Household storage systems

Plus 5 Interiors
1230 Yonge Street
Toronto, ONT
Canada M4T-1W3
(416) 923-5231
Furnishings, design consultation

Quaker Maid
Division of Tappan Corporation
Route 61
Leesport, PA 19533
(215) 926-3011
Kitchen and bathroom cabinetry

Rubbermaid Incorporated
1147 Akron Road
Wooster, OH 44691
(216) 264-6464
Office, kitchen, bath products

Rudd International Corporation
1025 Thomas Jefferson Street
Washington, DC 20007
(202) 333-5600
Stackable chairs and tables

Scandinavian Design, Inc.
127 East 59th Street
New York, NY 10022
(212) 755-6078
Furnishings

Schulte Corporation
11450 Grooms Road
Cincinnati, OH 45242
(513) 489-9300
Ventilated shelving systems

Sherwood Corporation
P.O. Box 519
Spring City, TN 37381
(615) 365-5453
Convertible sofas

Spacial Environmental Elements Ltd. (SEE)
118 Spring Street
New York, NY 10012
(212) 226-0038
Adjustable height tables,
furnishings, accessories

Studio Azzurro
2533 Yonge Street
Toronto, ONT
Canada M4P-2H9
(416) 485-3000
Furnishings

Sturdi-Craft Marketing East
200 Boylston Street
Chestnut Hill, MA 02167
(617) 969-4700
Modular storage systems

Sunar Hauserman
5711 Grant Avenue
Cleveland, OH 44105
(216) 883-1400
Office systems

Swaim Originals
P.O. Box 4147
High Point, NC 27263
(919) 885-6131
Modular seating

Tazbaz Galleries Ltd.
225 Lakeshore Road East
Oakville, ONT
Canada L6J-1H7
(416) 842-4460
Furnishings

Techline
Marshall Erdman & Associates
5117 University Avenue
P.O. Box 5249
Madison, WI 53705
(608) 238-6868
Wall systems and furnishings

Urban Mode
385 Queen Street West
Toronto, ONT
Canada M5V-2A5
(416) 591-8834
Closet systems, furnishings

Vecta Contract (Distributors of Beylerian)
1800 S. Great Southwest Parkway
Grand Prairie, TX 75051
(214) 641-2860
Furnishings, including the
Beylerian collection

Velux-America Inc.
P.O. Box 3268
Greenwood, SC 29648
(800) 241-5611
Skylights and roof windows

Velux-Canada Inc.
16817 Hymus Boulevard
Kirkland, QUE
Canada H9H 3L4
Skylights and roof windows

Window Modes/Modern Windows
D & D Building
979 Third Avenue
New York, NY 10022
(212) 752-1140
Shutters, shades, vertical blinds, drapes

Ziggurat Concept Inc.
251 King Street East
Toronto, ONT
Canada M4P-2H9
(416) 362-5900
Furnishings

INDEX